ROMAN HOLIDAY.

NGANGOM KAILASH

ISBN 979-888530188-6

This books is dedicated to those who never fails to love themselves and respect others, and to those who believes in themselves and never fails to give up....

yours lovely- Ngangom Kailash

Contents

Foreword *vii*

Preface *ix*

Acknowledgements *xi*

Prologue *xiii*

1. Memories 1
2. 17 3
3. Heartbreak 5
4. Yellow 7
5. The Prince 9
6. Roman Holiday 11
7. Mirror 13
8. Blue Heaven 15
9. 2003 17
10. December 19
11. That Girl 21
12. Aphrodite 23
13. Red Smile 25
14. 90's 27
15. Forever Love 28
16. Persephone 29
17. Fake 31
18. Tilted Statue 33
19. Red Perfume 35
20. Teardrops 37

Contents

21. Perfectionist 39

22. All In One 41

23. Burning Heart 43

24. Smile(i) 45

25. Smile(ii) 47

26. Smile(iii) 49

Thanks 51

Foreword

I gave a sneak peek of this book, to one of my friend and he loves it, he is desperate to read all of these, hope that's the case if u all read it..

Preface

If u ever feel weak, remember why did you hold so long..

Mainly as humans each one of us undergoes, mind fluctuations and happy yet terrible emotions..

THIS BOOK STARTS WITH A SIMPLE MEMORY.. RECALL WHAT WAS YOUR NOSTALGIC MEMORY..

hence, it goes..

Acknowledgements

I would love to thank my lovely old friends, parents and dictionary who helped me with this book..

Prologue

The story goes..

HAVE A FUN JOURNEY WHICH STARTS AND END WITHIN A FLICK OF TIME..

1. Memories

I kept my crystals of tears encapsulated within a jar,
It shines with love of faith and truth,
I fear will it turn into stones?
Can I cherish or just throw it,
I know each such dots makeup my heart filled with holes,
The depth of pain will be revived,
The smile will prevail with forgotten lies,
Will the hatred go?
I still remember the envy in heart,
Will it ever go?
Can it ever come back?
I wish....

2. 17

I am 17,
I cannot see clouds of grey,
I wish there is an utopia for me, where I will be trusted, loved, and beleived,
The song of wisdom seems boring,
Or will I ever be stubborn as I am?
Will my stubborn dreams ever be fulfilled?
Cause I love the funk, I have many daydreamers which are dumb like me,
They are full with ego,
Will they be remembered?
My suffocation is extreme, thinking about my path,
Will I ever feel like 17 when I will be 50?

3. Heartbreak

They say," Valid lies can save lives",
Though my trenched heart is attached to glory of faith,
I hope faith can change them,
Nothing seems to change makes me feel love is embedded beneath,
My teary eyes cannot fetch water of hope anymore,
With my mind saying it is a heartbreak; No true love exist,
I heard, one never succeed until one fails,
Is it so?
I wished Pistis was with me,
Days and nights just flicked like a tick of time,
Nothing seems to change but I will try..

4. Yellow

I saw it when I was 4; I grew up like tendrils wrap around it
Those simple layers of smile had a huge impact,
Those simple love, created a class wherein my heart lies,
Those simple ground crafted with paints of colours, which was meant for us to enjoy,
Those friendships are superiors to what I am living with,
Those diamond studded laugh can neither be replaced nor found,
Those yellow dress will always be remembered,
Those forgiveness is what I want after a clash,
I miss those hugs,
I will come if I....

5. The Prince

A simple yet gorgeous Jack, THE PRINCE exists,
They say, he is built up of lies,
But his face hides his hideous aura,
Soon, time passes like a flow of water,
Jack says, "A shark followed me" ,
they came to save him; which turns out to be bluff,
His mischief flunked the arena with negativity and disbelief,
His flattering face loses its value as a consequence of his attitude,
Hatred towards him rises, then
" Jack, THE PRINCE was assasinated" ,
Eveyone weeps with a relief,

6. Roman Holiday

It was noon, I saw red paints on pink lips,
Passing through the streets of Paris , I imagined was it a heaven,
Liking every profound instruments; visiting every shops,
Flowing with the wind, laughing with music, having a cuisine,
Roaming till night to visit the stars, meeting every each one,
A simple kiss to my friend Eiffel , and a wave of goodbye,
Then,
It was 12:45 a.m. , I thought it was truly like a "Roman Holiday" ..

7. Mirror

I found a mirror in the backyard,
Ripped with vines decorated by flowers, a domicile for bees,
A little sleek of sun falled on it makes it shine like a crystal,
My shaky hands grabbed to see it,
Out of curiosity, found it was a magical one,
I asked it, " Mirror, do you have something to say about me, "
To which he replied, " Lie down " ,
I trusted my instinct and lied down,
To which I found myself on bed,
" Was it a dream? " , Or just a travel of time,
Out of curiosity, I ran to my backyard,
There was no accomodation of that mirror nor was there any vine located,
I LAUGHED, " WAS THAT A DREAM?"

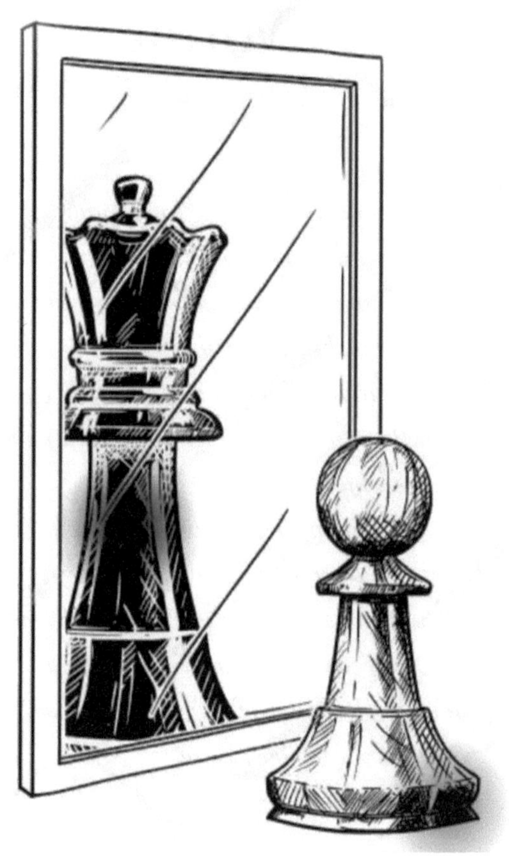

8. Blue Heaven

Will the sun shine, with love, with respect?
Will I ever feel lonely?
They say a blue sky has cherry trees, loving grasses, lovely unicorns,
They say it is a place of truth, a little droplets of calmness drops there,
Will I ever visit there?
Will that place exists?
They say a simple scent of red roses, and blue autumn leaves are waiting for me,
They say a blue heaven exists for people to feel safe, wherein, a butterfly can speak and fly,
Will they invite me?
Will I feel loved?

9. 2003

It was when I saw the living hell,
She told me, my eyes were like gold,
Every life starts with a cry,
She taught me crying is a form of rejuvenating,
I tried to mend stuffs,
The hard **December** , *saw me arriving,*
Mother Nature were evident cause they know,
I will come at 12:45 a.m.

10. December

The era of Christ's birth; the moment which embarked light,
The moment when snowflakes of different shades tripped on the window,
With glasses covered with lovely air, the arrival of Christmas,
The growth of holly and narcissus filled the arena with joys,
The love which spreads like nectar of such flowers,
The warmth is much more than what I thought,
I realised the generosity,
I love it,
The end of a great year..

11. That girl

She was a girl with two ponytails lift up,
A little bit of freckles, with a little fringes falling,
Her character was fed up with lack of belief,
She could not rise; despite that aura,
She falled with that two ponytails lift up,
Dirty was she, her angelic dress where ruined,
"Help" ....echoed
From nowhere, a God mother's voice emerged, She whispered,
'Don't fall, if you then, rise'
Has she understood it?
Time flicks, people said," That girl, was not confident though she is now",

12. Aphrodite

Embrace with jewels of nature; glistering shine sparkles from within,
Hands built of pure love, shredded by women of values,
She wears flowers embedded with diamonds, which spells the magic of L-O-V-E ,
With great beauty, she has her heart ready to serve,
She is one who knows moral of truth, the ambassador of humanity,
She is the majesty of Greek, the symbol of mystery,
Love resides in her eyes of fair smile,
Her beauty would not fade as time evolves..

13. Red Smile

Smudge face with hideous smile,
Reminds me of Princess Diana's death; a matter of sad,
Flickering mind fluctuates build up thoughts,
which consequently results in bad day,
A bad thought, a bad resut,
Such shades of red embarks threat to humanity,
Will they change?
It seems like a red smile..

14. 90's

Can you remember that greenery?
That mind with no hustle of losing,
A mind full of life, full of vitty,
The time got tons of love, huge respect,
Nor was I a 90's baby but can get a feel of it,
The fullness of life was a unique aspect of it..

15. Forever Love

A single smile, a single voice, reminds me of that;
That moment of joy, a single touch, reminds me of that;
That hugs of loveliness, a single courtesy, reminds me of that;
That freedom of speech, a single talk, reminds me of that;
That love she has for me..

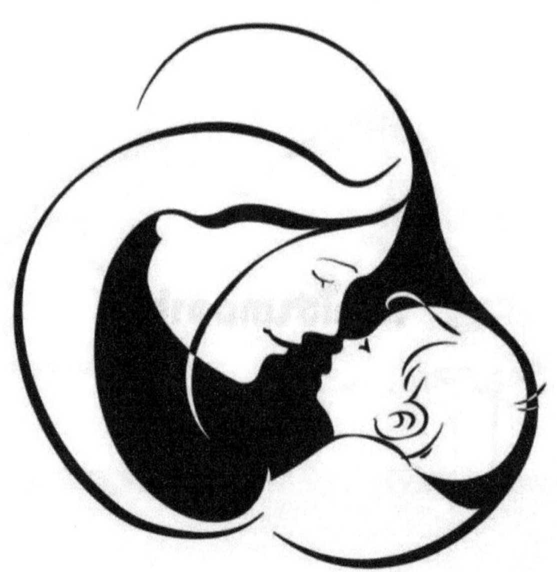

16. Persephone

She is the wife of Hades; the goddess of nature,
Her open smile brings in blooming flowers,
Her arrival is marked with grandeur opening,
Loving her is like loving a red wine,
It's worth increases with time,
Her departure consequences, the darkness and creepy coldness of our heart..

17. Fake

I saw that glory of that emperor,
I heard that he used to conquer everyone,
But is it true?
History is recorded in time, I cannot check it once,
If as money is power, then will it be justified?
If so, then will it ever be considered fake?
I think it should..

18. Tilted statue

Conquering valves with love,
Has won the trusts of many,
They loved him; loved his honesty, his faith,
The tame wind blew off the hard soil on his statue build with endeavour,
The staute lies alone on the sand,
which was once a preacher of everyone,
Things changes, time flies but history repeats..

19. Red perfume

Scent will become worthless; its everlasting aura will fade,
With envy of fake hearts, and pretty smile,
Gorgeous faces ruptures dark viscosity of bad blood,
A foolish individual guesses things with twice gestures,
But will he be able to guess, one with red perfume?
Red perfume hides away double looks, double chin,
Double thoughts, double smiles,
But it fades with time..

20. Teardrops

I saw a woman named nature crying,
Her story made me gasped and sigh at the same time,
The gorgeous woman used to laugh; I saw her smile full of glisters,
Someone said," People throw rocks at things that shine",
She heard my voice," why?",
She says," My domicile is destroyed",
My mind guess," why?",
OOh! She said cause of you..

21. Perfectionist

I have enough money to buy ten diamond rings,
But I could not help those in need,
I have wealthy cars enough to travel the world,
But I would not support them 'old people'
I have mind full of creativity,
But I could not support equality,
I have thousands of servants,
But I would not help the poor,
I am a perfectionist,
IS HE?

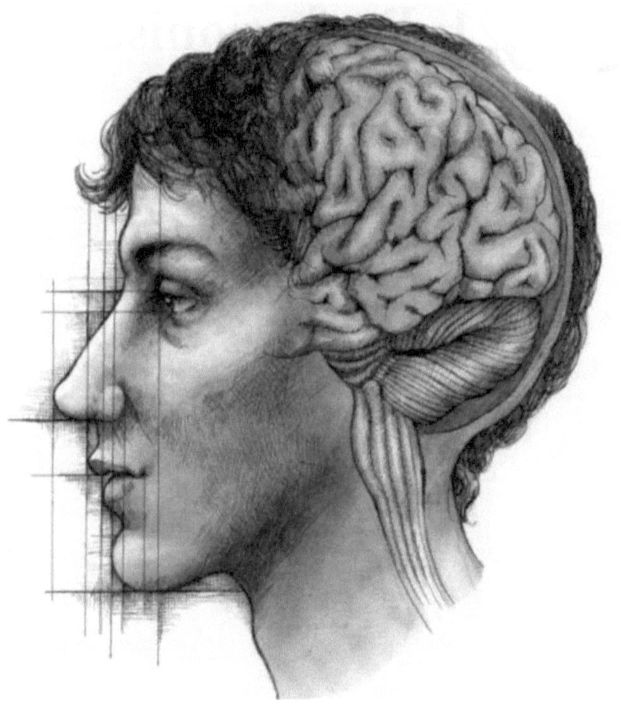

22. All in one

I knew not all are perfect,
But I want to share the love for them,
I want a room with curtains knitted,
with truthful passion, compassion,
little generosity, full of help, all in one,
I meant a curtain which seems like a rainbow, held by strength..

ROMAN HOLIDAY.

23. Burning heart

One magical night, I feel my heart burning out of pain, and ignorance,
It smells like a red perfume, and burns like a red wine,
It appears like a red rose filled with thorns, and reminds me of Roman Holiday,
It feels like a broken dreams,
It has an aura of bad witch's potion..

24. Smile(I)

My hands were runnig down to a paper,
thinking about that day,
It was cold yet calm,
The little yet prevailing costumes all over streets,
"HAPPY DIWALI" screamed someone; I guessed was that 'her',
The greets fluttered my pathway,
I guessed was that 'them'

25. Smile(II)

I, an introvert gasped the 'laugh' was good,
Giggling all the way; wishing my thoughts,
My feet was carried by wind,
Driven by people,
"I enjoyed the ride", I thought,
Others looking at my gestures,
They might be wandering,'OH!'

26. Smile(III)

The sweets tasted good, I shared with 'them',
They thanked, wished, congratulated,
"God, thank you", I prayed,
They were there happy, like me,
I hoped to see them,
My trail of life was carried by work,
Busy with, but wished it will happen again..

Thanks

BYE, Everyone thanks for taking your time and reading my thoughts written on a piece of paper,

hope that you have a magical day,

yours loving poet- Ngangom Kailash

Printed by Libri Plureos GmbH in Hamburg,
Germany